# Caught in the BLIZZARD

*a novel*

*by*

PAUL KROPP

 Dominie Press, Inc.

# Chapter 1

Sam raised the gun to his shoulder and looked along the sight. There it was—the herd of caribou he'd come to hunt. In his sight was a bull caribou, the largest in the herd. It was a huge animal. The bull had enough meat to feed Sam's brothers and sisters for a week or more. He pulled off one glove with his teeth and got ready to squeeze the steel-cold trigger.

"Wait," came a whisper from behind him. It was his grandfather's voice, rough from the cold.

Sam turned and looked at the old man. The face that stared back was much like his own: round and dark, with small, sharp eyes under heavy brows. But his grandfather's face had the deep wrinkles of sixty years. Sam's face was still that of a boy.

"Go closer," his grandfather whispered.

"They'll run off."

"Then they will come back," the old man said.

Sam shook his head. His old grandfather still hunted as in the old days, before guns had scopes that made the kill easy. But it was pointless to argue with him. Sam pointed the gun at the ground and walked slowly forward.

Just as Sam had predicted, the herd scattered away from them. But when he and his grandfather stood still for a few minutes, the herd became curious. They turned and came back. They came closer to study the two human figures outlined against the white snow and white sky.

Sam felt his grandfather's hand touch his arm. He turned and the old man nodded. The big bull caribou was close enough. Sam pulled off his glove and put his eye to the sight. He found the large bull and centered the sight on its shoulder. One shot, his grandfather always said. The kill will be quick for

the animal and certain for you.

Sam pulled the trigger. The gun exploded with a sudden flare from the barrel.

And the big bull caribou fell.

"One shot—good," his grandfather said. The old man was smiling. Half his teeth were gone, the other half black from chewing tobacco, but still he was smiling.

This was not Sam's first hunt. He'd been out on the land, the tundra, with his Grandfather Titus and his father since he was old enough to walk. But this was his first hunt with his own gun. The .22-250 rifle had been a sixteenth birthday present from his father. It was a beautiful gun. The barrel was still a shiny gray. The carved walnut handle didn't have a single scratch.

Sam knew the gun had cost a lot—more than his father could afford. But he had been given the gun anyway, and now it had brought down its first caribou.

Sam and his grandfather walked up to where the animal had fallen. The shot had been clean, right to the heart. The rest of the caribou was not damaged. A good kill, Sam thought. Perhaps a good omen.

His grandfather pulled out a knife, ready to skin the animal. But Sam held his hand back.

"I'll do it," Sam said.

His grandfather gave him a look. Both of them knew how little Sam liked to skin an animal. The kill was easy, but slicing into the still-warm flesh was hard. It was a job Sam had always left to the older hunters.

"I shot it, so I'll skin it," Sam said. His breath made clouds in the icy air. "It's time for me to start doing these things."

Sam knelt down onto the frozen snow and gently cut through the skin with his knife. He had gotten halfway through the skinning when he heard a roar. It was a snowmobile, coming their way.

Sam and his grandfather looked up. They stared at the growing spot of color on the horizon. It was coming from the east, from town. At the speed it was moving, the snowmobile would soon reach the herd.

At first the caribou took no notice of the

machine that was coming their way. They had run off at the blast of Sam's gunshot and then come back a little closer. Now they were just standing there, gray figures against the white snow.

But then the herd began to move. First one, then two, then all the animals began to run from the snowmobile.

"What is he doing?" asked Sam's grandfather. His eyes followed the bright red machine. "That is no way to hunt."

Sam and his grandfather watched as the snowmobile caught up to the panicking herd. They waited for the sound of shots, and for some of the caribou to fall. They knew that many of the young hunters in town came out like this, on snowmobiles, for a quick hunt. But still there were no shots.

"When will that man start to hunt?" asked Sam's grandfather.

"He isn't hunting," Sam replied. Now Sam knew what he was watching. The man on the snowmobile wasn't out to hunt the caribou. He wasn't out to feed a family, or even himself. He was out for "fun." He wanted to show off the power of his machine over these animals.

Off in the distance, the snowmobile began to slow down. It was right behind one of the caribou, a calf that was only half grown. The calf raced ahead, fleeing for its life, but the snowmobile stayed right behind it. The animal kept running, just ahead of the machine. It was a young caribou, a beautiful animal with much strength, but it was no match for the power of the snowmobile.

If there had been some question of who might win in all this, then a person might call it a sport. But there was no contest here. The young caribou ran steadily, turning back and forth. It was trying to outrun the snowmobile the way it might outrun a wolf. Five, ten minutes the chase kept on. Even in the distance, Sam could see that the caribou was losing strength and slowing down.

The animal turned and began running back toward Sam and his grandfather. The snowmobile turned, too, still chasing the calf. Now both the animal and the snowmobile grew larger as they approached.

The animal turned again to avoid Sam and his grandfather, and the snowmobile turned with it. The animal was close enough now that Sam could almost see the fear in its face. Fear was keeping it going; but the calf was losing strength with each minute.

In five minutes, the young caribou fell on its side. Its legs were still twitching, its lungs panting for breath. The person on the snowmobile slowed down for a look.

"The little caribou will die," Grandfather Titus said.

"That's the game," Sam replied. "Some guys think it's fun to chase them down like that."

"Fun?" asked the old man.

Sam didn't answer. He couldn't explain it, even to himself.

Hunting he could understand. The caribou and the Inuit had lived together for all time. The caribou grazed in the summer; the Inuit hunted in the winter. It was the age-old pattern, going back to the days before time. Even with guns, the Inuit still hunted to eat. Only in the 1950s did hunting

become a sport, after the new guns came. Then the hunting almost killed off all the caribou, and the Inuit starved on their lands. Now they knew better and no longer hunted, except for the meat of the animals.

But the young people were different—some of them. They watched videos and cable TV to learn the ways of the south. They no longer knew the nine words for snow, or the names of the elders who played games in the sky at night. But they knew swear words from Los Angeles and the names of the regulars on MTV.

Sam watched as the man on the snowmobile circled around the dying animal. Then there was a roar and the snowmobile took off, back toward the town. The rider was too far away for Sam to make out his face. But he recognized the bright red snowmobile. And he could guess who was riding it.

"You know the boy?" Sam's grandfather asked.

"Yes," Sam admitted. "It's Connor O'Brien." He felt embarrassed to know his name.

"He should be spoken to, but I don't know his family well," Grandfather Titus said softly.

"His father works for the airline," Sam said. "He doesn't care what Connor does."

The caribou herd regrouped, now that the snowmobile was gone. They gathered around the fallen calf. Perhaps they were angry in their silent way.

"We will have to shoot that caribou," grandfather Titus said. "A slow death is too cruel for any living thing."

"And stupid," Sam added. "I'll get the dogs and then shoot it."

"No, you finish skinning," said his grandfather. "You shouldn't use your new gun for this ..." His words trailed off. Sometimes Sam wondered what the old man was thinking when his words died away.

Sam knew his own thoughts. *Connor is an idiot,* Sam said to himself. *I'd like to see him struggling to survive out here on the snow.* Then he felt ashamed of his thoughts. He couldn't know that he had seen an image of the future. Nor could he know that he, too, would be fighting to stay alive on the frozen tundra.

# CHAPTER 2

Sam sat in The Coffee House after school with his friend Billy. They were sipping tea, which was Billy's favorite drink, after Coke. Coke cost a lot at The Coffee House—almost five dollars a can because it cost so much to bring it up from the south. But tea was cheap, so tea was what they drank.

The Coffee House was busy at four o'clock. Students from the high school had come in after their last class. Older men and women from Arctic College were sitting at two tables. Martin Ikiluk, the owner, was trying to cook hamburgers, pour hot water into teapots, and clean tables, all at the same time.

Sam and Billy knew everyone in the place, except a new girl who was sitting with a friend over in the corner.

"Who's that with Rachel?" Billy asked. He brushed his dark hair out of his eyes, and then looked right at the new girl.

"You shouldn't stare," Sam whispered.

"I'm just trying to see her a little better," Billy kept on, the way he always did. "She's pretty nice, I think. Just my type."

Sam shook his head. "You think every girl is your type. Maybe that's why none of them wants you for a boyfriend."

"So who is she? She looks *kabloona*," he said, using the word for *white person*. The girl had the straight dark hair and the dark skin color of Sam and Billy, but she also had a long nose and thin lips.

"Her name's Annie," Sam told his friend. "She's in my math class. I hear she came from Yellowknife last week to stay with her cousins. She was in some kind of trouble down there, at least that's what everybody says."

"What's she like?" Billy asked.

"Quiet," Sam replied. "She's smart, but she doesn't say much."

Billy smiled, showing his yellowed teeth. "So, you've got your eye on her already?" And then he laughed.

Sam just shook his head. Neither he nor Billy had a girlfriend, at least not right now. The girls seemed more interested in other kinds of guys—the flashy ones, the ones with money, the ones who could make jokes. Sam was too serious, too quiet, too shy. Billy acted too much like a kid, just like he looked. Maybe that's why he smoked cigarettes, to try to seem older.

Billy had just taken a smoke out of the pack when his eyes went to the door. "Guess who's just come in?" he said to Sam. "The great white hunter, so long as he's got his killer snowmobile."

Sam turned and saw Connor walk in and scan the room, looking for a place to sit. Connor was dressed, as always, in expensive jeans that his father bought down south and a ski parka that belonged at a resort, not in the Arctic. Connor had that funny smile on his face—the teacher called it a smirk—that always made him seem as if he were laughing at you.

"Uh-oh," Billy said. "He's got his eye on your girl Annie."

"She's not my girl," Sam began, but he stopped because it was useless to speak. Billy liked to make fun of Sam and his shyness. He'd been doing that ever since Sam could remember, and he wasn't going to stop with a quick word or two.

"Look at that," Billy whispered. "Talk about moving in fast!" Connor had already pushed himself into a table beside Annie and Rachel.

Sam just shook his head. Connor O'Brien had his pick of the girls at school. There was something about his California-style looks and his confidence that made girls fall all over him. Sam and all the other boys envied him, but that's just how it was.

"Hey, Sam," Connor said after ordering a Coke, "saw you out hunting with your dad on Saturday." Connor looked over to make sure the new girl was watching him—and she was. He turned to her. "He still goes out in a dogsled," he said, slapping himself on the head. "I mean, that was high-tech about two hundred years ago."

Annie, the new girl, lifted her cup of tea and hid her eyes.

"I was with my grandfather," Sam told him. "Our snowmobile's broken." Then he felt stupid for explaining himself to Connor.

"Your snowmobile's older than you are," Connor said, laughing as if he'd made a great joke. He turned to Annie, grinning at her. "Down south, that thing would be in a museum."

"It works okay most of the time," Sam mumbled, mostly to himself. He tried to look at Billy and ignore what Connor was saying. But Billy was busy staring at Connor and the new girl.

"Listen," Connor said to the new girl, loud enough for Sam and Billy to hear. "I could take you out on my new machine some day. Show you what a *real* snowmobile can do."

"I grew up in Yellowknife," Annie said quietly. "I've been on plenty of snowmobiles."

"And there's nothing so great about yours, Connor, except maybe its noise," Rachel piped up. "And how come you didn't ask *me* to go with you?"

Connor seemed a little embarrassed. "Well, it's just because Annie's new up here, you know. I didn't want her to think that all the guys are like those two beanbags." He nodded in the direction of Sam and Billy, and then made a face that got Rachel giggling.

Sam twisted in his chair, trying to ignore Connor's words, but he felt his temper rising.

Connor went on speaking to Annie. "I could take you out and show you how to hunt. Those caribou haven't got a chance when you've got a good snowmobile."

That's when Sam lost it. "What do you know about hunting?" he shouted across the restaurant. "All you do is chase down caribou with a machine."

Billy looked at his friend, surprised at his sudden anger.

"C'mon, Sam, lighten up," Connor replied. "You've been hanging out with the old folks too much. You take everything so seriously, man. You've got to get out and have a little fun."

Sam felt the heat rise up inside him. "You think you can chase an animal to death—all for fun?"

Everyone in the restaurant was staring now, almost waiting for a fight to break out between the two.

"Well, sure," Connor replied. The smile on his face disappeared.

"I think it's stupid," said Sam. He didn't speak like this, not to anyone, but Connor had pushed him too far.

"I think you'd better watch who you call stupid," Connor threatened. The look on his face turned menacing.

Sam stood up. He wanted to reach out and hit Connor, or slap him, or do something with his fists that he couldn't do with words. But Billy was up beside him, telling him to calm down. Then old Martin Ikiluk was yelling at them, saying he didn't want any trouble in his restaurant. In seconds, Billy was paying for the tea and grabbing their schoolbooks, and the two of them were out the door.

The cold air hit them like a slap in the face, but Sam's anger was slow to cool.

"I've never seen you get so mad," Billy said.

"I thought for a second you were going to hit him."

"I wanted to," Sam grumbled.

"But then Martin won't let us go in for tea anymore. I think this whole thing has really gotten to you, Sam. I mean, running down a caribou calf is stupid, but you're not the game warden. You've got to cool it, you know?"

"I know, I know," Sam admitted. He didn't need Billy to lecture him, now that the anger was going down. He shook his head and pulled his parka hood tight against the wind.

A three-wheeler went sputtering down the road. Off by the Northern Store, the town's one taxi was picking up someone to go off to the airport. On a slight rise near the bay, an ancient stone Inukshuk pointed the way into town.

"Sam?" Billy said.

Sam turned to his friend. "What?"

"That girl, Annie. All the time Connor was going on about his snowmobile, and even after that, she kept on looking at you."

"Really?" Sam felt embarrassed.

"Really," Billy replied.

"But if she falls for Connor, she's not worth the trouble, is she?"

"I don't know," Billy said. "She seemed pretty nice, nicer than most of the girls around here. If you ask me, I think you're just scared."

Sam stared at his friend and felt his anger rising again. "Connor doesn't scare me."

"Not scared of Connor," Billy said, grinning at his friend. "Scared of the girl!"

# CHAPTER 3

Sam pulled on a pair of caribou-hide wind pants, and then put on his heavy parka. It was a funny mix of old and new, just like so much of his life. The caribou wind pants had been made by his mother, as she had learned from her mother. The parka, on the other hand, came from the Northern Store: $129.95 on sale. It was made of polyester and Dacron and stitched together in China.

The whole outfit looked silly. But caribou hide was better against the wind than anything you could buy. If Sam could ever get a caribou-hide coat, like his father's, then he could handle the worst winter storm.

Sam was ready to go. He and Billy were going out on the land to hunt caribou. Grandfather Titus had told him of a large herd not far from town. And Billy wanted to use his family's snowmobile. Billy's dad had bought it secondhand, but Billy was still proud of it.

Sam just hoped the snowmobile wouldn't break down and leave them out on the land. In minus 40 degree weather, you could often stay alive for a few days until search and rescue found you. But if a blizzard came up, then you could get frostbite in minutes. Without shelter, you could be dead in a day. The Arctic, as Grandfather Titus often said, forgives nothing.

"You ready?" Billy asked. He was stomping off snow as he came to the hall.

"I need my gun," Sam told him. "Did you bring the rest?"

"Food, tent, shells, candy, smokes. I think I've got all the stuff you could want—except maybe that girl, Annie." Billy grinned at him.

Sam refused to smile back at Billy. Sam had seen Annie twice in class since that day at The Coffee

House, but she paid no attention to him. Still, Billy kept on bugging him about her.

Sam strapped his gun onto the *komatik*—the sled behind the snowmobile. Then he climbed onto the seat behind Billy. With a roar, the machine took off, up the little rise by Sam's house. Then they went down the snow-covered road. In minutes, they were onto the flat tundra outside of town.

"North," Sam said into the back of Billy's parka. "Up toward Old Abe's cabin."

Both of them knew this land. Their fathers, uncles, and grandfathers had taken them out since they were children. They knew the names for snow and the places to hunt. They knew where the fishing holes opened up in the summer and where the flowers would bloom in June.

It was the big world down south that was a mystery. Sam had once flown to Crater Lake for a basketball game. Billy had never been very far from town. But neither had ever been south to Seattle or Chicago. They saw these places on TV, on the news, but these were only pictures. This land, the frozen land of the caribou, was theirs.

"See anything?" Billy asked, turning back to his friend.

"Off to the right," Sam shouted. He searched the horizon for the caribou, tiny gray shapes against the sky.

"There's nothing," Billy said.

"No, but keep going," Sam told him.

Grandfather Titus seemed to have a sense for the animals. He could sense the caribou without seeing them. Even at his age, Titus could see them before Sam could. But Sam did not have that gift—only his two dark eyes.

"Over there," said Sam. "I see something."

So did Billy. Off on the flat snow there were a few dots of gray, maybe nothing more than shadows. But sometimes the bits of gray would turn out to be a whole herd of caribou. And then the hunting was easy.

Billy turned his snowmobile to the right. He dropped the speed slightly so the roar wasn't so loud. Up ahead, the gray dots grew larger. More and more, Sam thought they had found the herd. But something was wrong.

"They're not moving," he shouted to Billy.

"Yeah, that's funny," Billy called back. "And there's something else."

From where they were, the two boys couldn't see the "something else." But as they got closer, the horror became clear. The gray shapes of the caribou became separate animals, each lying on the ground.

The grim scene up ahead made them fall silent. There were fourteen caribou lying on the ground.

The blood had surged out of their bodies, staining the snow. Then the bodies were quick-frozen in the Arctic cold, never to move again.

Animal after animal, it was the same. They had been shot in the head, the gut, the leg. Some had died on the spot and fallen fast. Others had run until the blood drained away. Then they, too, had fallen and died.

But when they looked more closely, the boys could see that the horror was still worse.

"They've been cut," Billy said. He turned off the snowmobile. Now the two of them stood in the middle of the dead herd. Around them were the sliced-open bodies of the caribou.

"Someone wanted the antlers," Sam said. He walked over to one dead animal and knelt down beside it. It was as cold as the ice. He looked at the wound that had killed the caribou, then at the ripped flesh where the antlers had been.

There was a pool of blood from the mouth as well, frozen against the snow. The tongue had been cut out.

Sam and Billy knew what this meant. These

caribou had been killed not for food, but for cash. The tongues were worth good money in Japan; the antlers would be ground up and sent to China.

"What do we do?" Billy asked.

"Nothing," Sam answered. The frozen bodies could no longer be skinned. The blood had been left inside, so they were useless as meat.

"But someone…"

"I know. Someone wanted to make money. Someone who has a way to get the tongues and antlers out of town." Sam got up and looked at the angry sky.

"It must be Connor," Billy said. "His father…"

Sam didn't let him finish. "Now we know how he bought that new snowmobile," Sam said.

"But we haven't got any proof," Billy said.

"I'm going to get proof," Sam told his friend. "I'm going to stop Connor if it's the last thing I do."

# CHAPTER 4

The next time Sam and Billy came into The Coffee House, they saw Connor at a corner table, close beside Annie. He had his big white boots propped up on a chair.

Sam held back at the door. "Maybe we should just go to my house," he said. "I don't want trouble." Sam knew his anger came up very suddenly. Maybe that's why he was so quiet, always pushing down the emotions he couldn't control.

"Oh, come on," Billy replied. "That basketball practice made me thirsty, and I want something to drink. Who cares about them? You're not jealous of that jerk, are you?"

"No, not me," Sam said quickly. Everyone at school already knew that Connor and the new girl were going together. "It's just the caribou herd…" Sam said, his words falling away.

"You said yourself—there's no proof. And what could we do, even if there were?" Billy whispered.

Billy was right, of course. Sam had spoken to his family when he got home from the hunt, but there was nothing to do. Grandfather Titus had already gone to see Connor's father about that day with the snowmobile. But Connor's father didn't care. He had just laughed when the old man spoke about "respect" and "teaching your son how to hunt."

Connor's father didn't care about hunting. He made his money handling bags at the airport. He rarely hunted, and when he did, it was only for fun. The food the O'Brien's ate came from the Northern Store, or right off the plane. If Connor wanted to have a little fun, said Mr. O'Brien, why should he care?

"I don't like this," Sam grumbled as they both sat down. Billy had taken a table on the other side of the restaurant. But The Coffee House was so small that they couldn't help but hear.

"You shoot a polar bear with a .257," Connor said loudly. "Anything less won't stop it. Last time I did it, of course, the bear kept on coming."

"That must have been dangerous," Annie replied, her eyes wide. She was looking at Connor as if he were the greatest hunter on earth.

"It was," Connor went on, proud of himself.

"I only had one shot left, so if I missed—well, I wouldn't be sitting here with you."

"So your second shot stopped the bear?"

"My second shot was perfect. Right to the hip. You don't want to shoot the head, because then the skin isn't worth much. But my shot was right where I aimed it. I wasn't shaking or anything. I just took careful aim, squeezed the trigger and…"

"And then you woke up," Billy called out.

Everyone in the restaurant broke into laughter.

Connor turned, saw Billy, and stood up. In a second, he was over at the table where Billy and Sam sat with their tea.

"Am I going to have trouble with you, too?" Connor spat out. His hands were already tightened into fists.

"C'mon, Connor," Billy told him. "You've never hunted a polar bear in your life. My uncle has. Sam's grandfather has. But you have to have your name drawn in the lottery. No one in your family has ever been that lucky."

Billy just stared up at him. Sam could tell that Billy was afraid but trying hard not to let it show.

What Billy had said was true. Only twelve polar bears a year could be hunted. Everyone in town put their name in the lottery to see whether they would be allowed to hunt. Only twelve names were drawn. Everyone knew who had won the chance, and who hadn't.

"You think I care about the lottery?"

"I think you ought to care," Sam spoke up. "Or are you telling all of us that you broke the law?"

Connor backed off when he looked around the room. "I'm not saying anything. I'm just…"

"Shooting your mouth off," Billy finished for him. "Now go back and tell Annie some more stories. Maybe you can fool her, but the rest of us know the truth."

Connor came back, furious. In a second, he had

grabbed Billy by the coat and lifted him up. He spat in his face. "You little…"

But before Connor could say another word, there were ten hands pulling him away from Billy. Sam had been the first to push Connor back. Now Martin Ikiluk was between Connor and Billy.

"Out, all of you. Out of my place," he ordered. "You're all trouble. Nothing but trouble."

"And you're an old—" Connor swore.

For a second, Sam thought that Martin Ikiluk might actually hit Connor. The old man was that angry, but others in the restaurant held their tempers. With some shouting and pushing, the angry teenagers were sent out the door.

Billy fell to the snow, Connor standing above him.

"I ought to punch your stupid face in," Connor kept on.

Billy just stared up at him. He was small, but he had dealt with bigger guys than Connor.

"For what? For telling the truth?" Billy shot back.

"Could you two just stop it?" Annie broke in.

She was trying to get into her coat and boots all at once. "Connor, I don't care about all this. I wanted to leave this kind of thing back in Yellowknife. Forget it. It's all over."

"She's right," Sam said. "It's finished." He looked at the others and wondered at how quickly the anger had blown up.

"This isn't over," Connor kept on. "Nobody calls me a liar to my face and just walks away."

"He didn't call you a liar," Sam said. "He said you tell stories. Why don't you tell Annie stories about the way you really hunt."

"What?"

"Billy and I found that herd of caribou you slaughtered. Was that fun, too, cutting the tongues out? Did you get really big bucks for the antlers?"

Connor was quiet for a moment. "I don't know what you're talking about," he said.

"Right," Billy said, his voice dripping with sarcasm.

"We know, Connor," Sam said, shaking his head. "We can't prove it yet, but we know."

"Connor, what are they talking about?" Annie asked.

Now all three of them were staring at Connor, and the boy blushed. His anger was gone, and now something like shame showed in his face.

"Nothing, it's nothing," he said. "I don't know what they're talking about. They're crazy."

Annie looked at Billy and Sam as if to check out how crazy they were. Then she turned back to Connor. "I think it's time you took me home."

Connor turned and walked with her to the three-wheeler. Billy and Sam shook their heads, heading north along the dark street. They were both in trouble now—with Martin Ikiluk, and then with their families when word got back. And why? Was it because of the caribou? Or because of a girl named Annie?

# CHAPTER 5

There was no more trouble, at least for a while. Sam and Billy went to school and tried to stay away from both Connor and Annie. Midterm exams were coming up, so it was time to do some studying.

What surprised them both was that Connor didn't come after them. They didn't see him for almost a week, and even then he didn't pay much attention to them. It was as if the whole problem at The Coffee House had been forgotten. Or maybe it wasn't as important as other things on his mind.

Sam had a hunch that the police might be worrying Connor a little. When Grandfather Titus reported the cut-up caribou herd, Sam didn't expect much to happen. But the police seemed to take it very seriously. At least the officer wrote down everything Sam told him. What Sam didn't mention was the person he suspected of the crime. *Let that come from somebody else*, Sam had said to himself. *I've had trouble enough.*

The cops aren't stupid, Billy pointed out. They could figure the whole thing out easily enough. The problem was getting proof. Rumors would often zoom around a small town like theirs, but proof was slower to surface—and harder to pin down.

Sam had planned to go hunting on Saturday, but he had to put that plan off. A blizzard warning had come in the night before. The last thing Sam needed was to get caught out on the tundra in a blizzard. Besides, there was work to do at home: new drywall in one bedroom, paint in the living room. And he had a history project due.

The tundra would still be there after the storm had passed. Then it might be safe to take the dogs and go out hunting.

So Saturday morning, Sam was putting up

drywall tape when Grandfather Titus came in from feeding the dogs.

"It's going to be bad, a real *piqiq*," said the old man, using the Inuit word for *blizzard*. He had taken Sam by surprise.

"How do you know?" Sam asked. "Do you know how to read the clouds, or is there some special sign you look for?"

Grandfather Titus shook his head. "No, I listened to the forecast on the radio. I could teach you how to do that." The old man smiled, revealing his missing teeth. "First, you turn the radio on."

"Grandpa," Sam groaned. Then he went back to work with the drywall tape.

An hour later, Sam had spread drywall paste on the tape, the floor, his fingers and—somehow—his nose. Outside, the storm had begun. The winds tore at and under Sam's house, snow pelting hard against the windows. If the *piqiq* got any worse, travelers would hardly be able to see their own boots as they tried to find their way home.

Sam had just about finished the drywall work when he heard someone knocking at the door. He was surprised. Even a walk down the street could be dangerous in a blizzard.

"Sam," his mother called. "It's somebody for you."

Sam grabbed a rag to wipe away some of the drywall paste and came out of the bedroom. He thought it might be Billy, his partner on the history project. But the figure in the front hall wasn't that of his friend.

"Annie?" Sam felt stunned.

"I need some help," Annie told him. She was dressed in her parka and boots, already covered in snow.

"Help? Who?" Sam asked. By now, all five of his brothers and sisters were peeking down the hall at Annie. He knew his parents and Grandfather Titus, too, would be listening hard.

"It's Connor," she explained. "He went off this morning, early, before the storm. He said he'd be right back."

"Why'd he go off on a day like this?" Sam asked. "Doesn't he listen to the radio? Doesn't he know anything?"

Annie looked down at the floor. "Look, don't lecture me, okay? It wasn't my idea."

"Sorry," Sam said, embarrassed by his own temper. "What do you want me to do? We should call Search and Rescue and tell them he's out in the storm."

"My aunt did that already," Annie told him. "They're not going to send out a search party in this storm unless they know he's lost. He's only been gone for three hours."

"So, how do you know he's lost?"

"Because I know where he was going. And I know he should have been back already. He needs help."

Sam shook his head. This girl had to be out of her mind. They were having the worst storm of the year, and she was asking him to go find a guy who was his enemy. Besides, Sam's snowmobile was still broken, and the dog team had just been fed. The dogs would be sleepy and slow after their meal. Going out with the dog team in this storm would be just plain stupid.

Annie could see him shaking his head, so she

gave her effort one last shot. "I need somebody who's smart enough to help me find him in the storm."

Sam felt embarrassed. How could she do this to him with just a word or two? "Smart or crazy?" he asked.

"Both, I guess."

There was a silence. Sam looked at the floor. Annie stared down the hallway at the ten eyes that were peeking around doorways at her. Outside, the winds roared like giant animals fighting up above the roof.

"No, it's just crazy," Sam concluded.

Annie looked down, embarrassed for having asked. "Never mind then. I'll go myself." Her voice sounded as cold as the wind outside.

Sam stood there, stunned, as she turned and went outside. The bitter wind slammed the door tight.

When Sam could focus again, what he saw was Grandfather Titus's face. The old man was silent, but his eyes asked a serious question. It was the question Sam was asking himself.

Sam needed only a few seconds to make his decision. Then he pulled open the door and yelled into the snow-choked air.

"Annie, wait! I'll get the dogs. Wait up!"

# CHAPTER 6

The dogs began barking as Sam and Annie approached them. They barked at Sam because they thought he might feed them again. They barked at Annie because she was a stranger.

"You're not dressed for this," Sam muttered. Annie was dressed for the south: ski jacket, light boots, ski gloves, and wind pants. None of that would last long against the biting cold and fierce wind out on the Arctic tundra.

"It's what I've got," Annie snapped at him.

"Go in the house and see my mother while I set up the sled. Tell her you need some caribou pants and gloves like mine."

"I'll be fine," Annie said.

"No you won't," Sam countered. Then he raised his eyes to hers. "Please?"

Annie mumbled something and went back into the house. Sam began putting a harness on each dog. He felt nervous, already, and not just because of the blizzard. There was something about that girl Annie that got under his skin.

It took ten minutes to get the dogs harnessed and tied to the *komatik*, or sled. Sam could have done it faster, except for the wind and the cold. Finally the team and sled were ready, all eight dogs straining against their leads. But where was Annie? This whole thing had been her idea, and now she had disappeared. Sam was about to go off to the house to look for her, when he heard her voice.

"Let's go," she called. "I'm ready."

Sam could see her dim shape getting clearer as she got closer. It was Annie, but now she was dressed in clothes for the tundra: caribou pants, jacket, and gloves. She looked more like an Inuk than Sam did.

"Your mother said this stuff would keep me

48

warmer," Annie said. "She even gave me some stuff in case we get stranded—bannock and matches and a Thermos of coffee."

"We won't get stranded," Sam replied, though in his heart he wasn't quite so sure.

"You know, Sam, your mom's pretty nice," Annie snapped. "Too bad you're not more like her."

It took a second for the insult to strike home, and then Sam felt as if he'd been slapped. Nice? He was plenty nice. Just who was going out on this crazy rescue mission, anyhow?

"Sorry," Annie mumbled as she climbed onto the *komatik*. "I didn't really mean it. I don't know why I say things like that." She pulled the snow goggles down over her eyes.

Sam didn't know what to say, but the dogs were ready and Annie was ready, so there seemed to be no reason to speak. He lifted the anchor, threw it into the sled and climbed on. The dogs pulled Sam and Annie away from the town, away from the warmth of the houses, out toward the vast tundra.

"Where to?" Sam shouted back to Annie.

"Out by Martin Ikiluk's camp," she told him.

"Then I can show you where to go after that."

"What's out there?" Sam asked

"Another camp," she shouted. "Connor and his father use it to…" Annie's words died out in the wind and snow.

Sam was surprised. He didn't know that Connor's family had a camp, but now he had a hunch what it might be used for. They had to have someplace to keep the caribou antlers and tongues until the plane took them out. A camp way out beyond Martin Ikiluk's would be perfect.

But how did Annie know about it? Was she part of the whole smuggling deal, too? Images of Annie and Connor at the camp kept coming into Sam's mind. *Don't think about that*, he told himself. *Drive the dog team.*

Annie had one thing right: Sam knew about the land. Even in the blizzard, Sam and his dogs could find their way. The lead dog, Queenie, could find her way on the land when a person would be lost in a wall of white.

It took twenty minutes to get to Martin Ikiluk's camp. The camp was buried under new snow when

51

they got there. It looked more like a graveyard than a camp, a thought that made Sam shiver.

"Now where?"

"Keep going straight," Annie shouted.

Sam called out to the dogs, "Go!" They had been slowing down for the past few minutes. Maybe the dogs were wondering whether there really would be meat for them at the end of the run. Or maybe they sensed a real danger in the storm. "Faster!" Sam ordered, shaking the leads.

The dogs obeyed, pulling Sam and Annie into the white wall of air. The snow was still coming hard, the wind blowing it into their faces. Up ahead there was nothing to see: white snow on the ground, white snow in the air, and white air beyond that.

Sam felt tiny pinpricks in his spine. If they got into trouble, the dogs could find their way home, but still there was a hint of fear nagging at him. Maybe it was the fact that Annie was with him now, that it wasn't just him out on the tundra. Or maybe it was that the land ahead of them was so white, so cold.

"How far?" Sam shouted.

"Not very far—it only takes five minutes on the snowmobile."

That would be ten, maybe twenty minutes by dog team. Sam couldn't be sure they'd even see the camp through the wind-driven snow. The storm had covered all snowmobile trails and turned any signposts into white figures against a white sky.

"Will you know the place?"

"If I see it," Annie shouted.

Sam yelled at the dogs, driving them on. After ten minutes of this, he shouted at them again, and then threw out the anchor.

"Why are we stopping?" Annie asked.

"To look," Sam said. It seemed silly, of course, trying to look into the white wall of snow and air, but it gave Sam a chance to clear away the snow from his goggles and his face.

"Does this look close?" Sam asked.

"I don't know. I've never been out in a storm! It all looks the same," Annie replied.

"I'm going to slow down the dogs and move around a little. Keep your eyes open."

Sam lifted the anchor, and the dogs began

pulling again. He shouted ahead, "tch-tch," to move them left, a quick whistle to move them right. They began zigzagging as they moved forward, looking for something. Anything.

"What's that?" Annie shouted.

"What's what?"

"Up ahead. See, it's a little darker. That shape."

Sam could see the dark form as they drew closer. It wasn't a camp. It was too small for that, and it had too much color—red color.

"It's Connor's snowmobile!" Annie cried.

She was right again. Sam guided the dogs up beside the half-buried snowmobile, and then threw out the anchor. He and Annie climbed off the sled and went over to the snowmobile.

"Connor!" Annie shouted out, but there was no reply, just the roar of the wind batting against them.

Sam took off his glove and touched the red snowmobile. Its engine was cold, and the machine was covered with snow. It must have been sitting here, broken, for more than an hour.

"Here's what happened," Sam said, kneeling

beside the machine. "The track broke."

"Can you fix it?" she asked.

"Not out here. Connor probably tried to go on to the camp, and he might even be there by now."

Annie smiled. "So he'll be all right."

"Unless the wolves got him first," Sam muttered.

Annie's smile disappeared. "Let's go," she said. "We'll keep going until we find him."

Sam felt stupid for saying what he'd said. No wolf or bear would be out above ground in a storm like this. If Sam had had any sense, he wouldn't be out, either. But his words had kept the search going, so now the two of them climbed back onto the *komatik*. Sam lifted the anchor and shouted for the dogs to pull the sled off into the snowstorm.

They hadn't gone even two minutes before Annie cried in Sam's ear. "Wait!"

Sam turned quickly, threw out the anchor, and turned to face Annie. "Do you see the camp?" he asked.

"No, I saw something. I don't know what."

Sam shook his head. The snow was coming

down harder, making it tough to see anything at all. White against white—shades of white from snow to air to sky—but that was all.

"Where was it?" Sam asked.

"Back up a little," Annie told him. "Come on."

She was off the sled before him, trudging back through the snow. Sam followed, convinced that she was crazy—that this whole thing was crazy.

"Up ahead!" Annie cried out.

And then Sam could see. Up ahead, on the snow, was a spot of color. It wasn't the natural colors of the north, the whites and grays and browns of the land. It was the glowing red of a Northern Store parka. Sam and Annie both began to run. At last, they'd found Connor.

## CHAPTER 7

Connor was lying face down on the ground when they reached him. Snow had half-covered his parka and wind pants. When Sam knelt down and lifted one shoulder, he didn't know if Connor was still alive.

"Oh no, oh no," Annie kept repeating, over and over again.

The face they saw was pale, drained of color. Connor wasn't moving, and his eyes weren't open.

"He's not…" Annie couldn't say what she was thinking.

"No," Sam said as he bent low over Connor. There was just a trace of warm breath on his cheek.

"He's alive." Sam pulled his hand from his glove and touched Connor's cheek. "I think he must be in some kind of shock."

"Your mom gave me a Thermos of coffee, just in case," Annie said.

"Bring it. There's a chance."

Annie ran back to the *komatik* and grabbed the small Thermos. When she returned, Sam had already lifted Connor up to a half-sitting position. Connor was still unconscious, but at least he didn't look like a dead body.

"Hold his mouth open and I'll give him some coffee," Annie said.

Sam did as she told him. The coffee splashed into Connor's mouth, then down his chin and onto Sam's coat. For a second, the coffee did nothing. Then Connor began to choke, spitting the coffee back up, over himself and Sam.

"What the…" Connor finally spoke.

"It's all right," Annie said. "Sam and I found you in time."

"Who? What?" Connor was still only half-conscious. He didn't seem to know where he was,

or how he got there, or why he was being held in Sam's arms.

"The track on your snowmobile broke," Sam told him.

A dim memory seemed to come back to Connor. Then he made a face, as if a sudden pain had shot through him. "My arm. It's broken. I can't move it."

"It's okay," Sam said. "We'll get you back to town, and the doctor can fix that. Can you walk?"

"Yeah, yeah," Connor said, pulling himself free of Sam. But the pain in his arm made Connor's face tighten.

"Here, drink the rest of the coffee," Annie said.

Connor slurped the coffee, the steam rising up from the Thermos cup. It seemed to revive him. "Did you call Search and Rescue?" he asked. Sam thought it was a strange question.

"No, it's just us," Annie told him.

Sam looked at Annie and frowned. "I thought you said you called Search and Rescue, but they wouldn't go out in this blizzard."

Annie looked away. "Come on," she said. "The storm is getting worse. We'd better get back to town."

Silently, Sam helped Connor to his feet, but he was strong enough to walk without much support. A broken arm was really his only problem, now that he was over the shock. Connor held the broken arm with his good one, trying to keep it from moving and causing still more pain.

When the three of them got back to the sled, they found the dogs huddled together against the cold. Sam spoke to them sharply, and they got ready to go. They were growling and barking at each other and at Connor. Sam tried to calm them down and untangle their leads while Annie and Connor got onto the sled.

Sam climbed onto the front of the sled, fitting himself between Connor's legs. He tried not to lean back against the broken arm and cause Connor further pain. Annie pulled up the snow anchor, Sam called out to the dogs, and they were off.

"Can't this go faster?" Connor shouted into Sam's ear. "I'm freezing."

"The dogs are tired," Sam said. "They do what they can."

Connor wouldn't let up. "Why didn't you bring a snowmobile? We could all freeze to death before we get back on this thing."

Sam was angry again. He had come all this way in a blizzard to save someone he didn't even like— an enemy—and now he was being treated like this. "Look, if you don't like it…" Sam began, but the words failed him.

"Would you two just stop it," Annie shouted

from the back. "Connor, you really are an ——," she said, swearing at him.

"What did you call me?" Connor said, shifting his weight to face her.

"Don't do that," Sam called out, but it was already too late. Just as Connor turned, the *komatik* hit a rock hidden under the snow. The force of the rock was enough to send the sled flying up into the air. Connor's shift at the back made the whole sled unstable.

"Wait!"

"Don't!"

"Oh, no!"

Then they were flying off the sled, all three of them. Annie went sailing off first. Then Connor grabbed at Sam to hold on, but he only managed to pull Sam off, too. In seconds, the three of them were lying in the snow, groaning in pain and spitting in anger.

"My arm!" Connor shouted in both anger *and* pain.

"You jerk!" Annie cried. "This is all your fault."

"It wasn't me. Sam should have seen the rock.

My arm! I swear it's broken twice!"

Sam was a little dazed at first, as if he'd hit his own head against a rock. But when the words between Annie and Connor became clearer, it wasn't the fighting that bothered him. It was the missing *komatik*.

"Where are those stupid dogs, Sam?" Connor demanded.

"I can't see them anywhere," Annie said.

Nor could Sam, but he knew why. "If the sled had tipped over, the anchor would have stopped the dogs. Now they'll keep going right back to town."

"How far do you expect me to walk with my arm like this?" Connor asked.

Sam shook his head. "We don't have to worry about walking," he told them. "We've got to worry about staying alive until somebody finds us."

# CHAPTER 8

"This is a stupid way to die," Connor kept saying, over and over again. "Stupid, stupid, stupid!"

There was nothing much that Sam could do to stop Connor's muttering. Nor could he help with the fear that lay underneath his words. Connor wasn't used to the tundra or the freezing cold of the Arctic winds. He was used to roaring out on his snowmobile, taking what he wanted, and then racing back to the warmth of his house. Now they had no snowmobile, and even the dogsled was gone. What little warmth they had wouldn't last long in the storm.

"Shut up," Annie said, giving Connor a shove. "Shut up and do something."

"Do what?" Connor whined. "It's Sam's dogs that did this."

Annie stared at him, the wind blowing in her face. "It's always somebody else, isn't it? Always. So who made you come out today? And how come I was so stupid that I came out after you? You're such a jerk. I should have been smart enough to see that from the start."

Sam stepped between the two of them. "Enough," he said. "We have to find some shelter against the wind, that's all. The Search and Rescue team will find us sooner or later."

There was a pause while Annie looked up, about to speak. "Nobody called Search and Rescue," she said at last.

Sam stopped and looked at her with a question in his eyes.

"I lied," Annie told him. Her face was wet from—was it melting snow? "I didn't want Search and Rescue to know about the camp. They'd find the antlers and everything."

"Don't tell him about all that," Connor said, cutting her off. "Nobody has to know."

Annie ignored Connor and kept on talking to Sam. "You shouldn't ever trust me," she said in a small voice. "I lie, I cheat, I do stupid things. That's why I got sent up here."

Sam looked at her, surprised. The rumors had been flying about Annie, especially since she had started going out with Connor. There were stories about her getting into trouble with some guy down south, doing drugs, dropping out of school. Nobody in town knew how many of the stories were true, but that didn't stop people from talking.

"Listen, it'll be all right," Sam told her. "My parents will call Search and Rescue if we're not back pretty soon. But we'd better get started building a shelter, just in case." Sam looked off at the clouds rolling in and felt the frozen wind blowing against him.

"Build a shelter with what?" Connor laughed. "Our bare hands?"

Sam's heart sank. There had been a snow knife back on the dogsled. It had the perfect blade to carve the hard snow into blocks. But the *komatik* was racing back to town with the dogs, and Sam had nothing.

"I've got a knife," Annie said, suddenly. She reached beneath the heavy caribou-hide coat and brought out a large switchblade.

"Where'd you get that?" Sam asked.

"I used to need it, down south," she said. "I started hanging around with a rough crowd, you know?"

Sam didn't know, but he was glad to see the knife. It gave them a chance—just a small chance—to survive.

The three of them fell silent as the wind howled harder than before. The tundra stretched out before them, cold and flat. Sam searched the white snow and ice, trying to find someplace where they could build shelter for the night.

And there it was—a small hump covered with snow, just off to the right. It looked like a large rock or a pile of rocks, not quite as tall as a man, but tall enough. It would give them one wall for their shelter.

"Over there. Come on!" Sam told them. He led

the other two off toward the spot he had seen, praying that they could build a shelter in time.

"What do we do?" Annie asked.

"We have to dig down into the snow, here, away from the wind. We cut the snow with the knife and then pile up the blocks."

"That's not a snow knife," Connor said, as he sat useless on the frozen ground. "This'll never work."

"Shut up," Annie said to him sharply. "I'll cut," she told Sam, "and you pile them up." Then she took the knife and began cutting into the snow.

People from the south have never seen such snow: dry and hard, but solid enough to build a wall against the wind. The Arctic snow had its own set of names, its own gods and legends. It has been both a friend and an enemy, depending on a man's skill and his strength. Or a woman's.

"Can you cut them bigger?" Sam asked.

"I'm doing the best I can," Annie called back, her voice tired. "How deep do you want me to go?"

"The deeper the better," Sam shouted. "Use two cuts, maybe. Or here, you stack up and I'll cut."

Annie agreed to the switch. Her arm was aching

from trying to hack at the frozen snow with a knife that was half the size of what they needed. In truth, Sam didn't do much better with the knife than Annie had done. The cutting and the building were a slow job, a block at a time, until finally they had dug down to the level of their knees. Sam climbed into the hole with Annie and stomped down a floor. Their shelter was halfway built.

"You should get in," Sam shouted to Connor. "You'll be warmer."

Connor grumbled, but soon climbed into the hole in the snow. It was better for him that way, with the wind blocked on three sides. Now Sam and Annie just had to finish the rest of the igloo, the way Grandfather Titus had shown him years ago. Titus could build a whole igloo, himself, in two hours. The last time Sam had tried to build one, it had taken him twice that long. But from the look of the clouds, they didn't have much time before the snow would bury them.

Quickly, Sam began cutting blocks of snow from the surface around them. Annie kept building up the igloo, stacking the new blocks on top of the

low walls Sam had made before. The important thing was to cover the top, so they wouldn't lose heat during the night. An opening further down could be blocked from inside.

"Are you trying to bury me?" Connor called out. The walls had arched up around him—against the rocks at one end, up from the snow at the other.

"Yes," Sam shouted back. In a way, that's just what they were doing. Sam and Annie were busy chinking the snow blocks, filling the cracks with handfuls of snow to cut the force of the wind.

The wind was the greatest danger. The snow might bury them, but the wind could freeze their bodies in a few minutes. With each minute, it was blowing harder, and then the snow got heavier.

"That will have to do," Sam cried to Annie as the heavy flakes of snow blew into his eyes. "Let's get inside."

The two of them climbed through the small "door" of their igloo, and then squeezed in beside Connor.

Connor was still grumbling. "We're going to freeze to death, and you've dug the grave yourself," he muttered. .

"We're not going to die," Sam snapped back. He was tired—tired of cutting and building and listening to Connor. "The igloo will hold the heat in and keep the storm out. If we had more food, we could last for a week like this. I think we can last until morning."

"Morning?" Annie asked. Her voice sounded muffled inside the snow shelter.

"It's late," Sam said. "Search and Rescue won't come out after dark, not in this storm. They'll find us tomorrow."

"What if the blizzard doesn't let up?" Annie asked.

"Then the next day," Sam said.

"If the wolves don't get us," Connor moaned. "If we don't freeze to death first. If we don't starve or get buried under the snow."

Neither Annie nor Sam wanted to hear any more. The makeshift igloo was enough, Sam thought, to keep them alive for one night. After that, the odds against them were much, much worse.

## CHAPTER 9

When Sam woke up, it was the middle of the night. His legs felt numb from the cold snow beneath them. The sky through the hole in the snow-block wall was black, but that meant the storm was over. Outside the wind had died down, the awful howling had finally stopped.

Inside the igloo, he felt Annie beside him, breathing softly in sleep. Connor was beside her, curled into her for warmth. If they'd had a *kudlik*, an oil lamp, they would have had a source of heat and light. Without it, the igloo was so dark, he could hardly see. But now that the wind had died down, it was easy to hear.

"You, no!" Annie cried out, lost in a nightmare. Her breathing stopped for a second, and then began again. In the dim, reflected moonlight, Sam saw Annie's eyes open wide.

"It's all right," Sam said, his voice a soothing whisper.

Annie said nothing for the longest time, but Sam knew she had not gone back to sleep. Her breathing was harsh, as if she were having another nightmare. When she finally spoke, her words were shaky. "I had a dream about dying," she told him.

"Sometimes I do, too," Sam told her. "Death is always close by, but it may not be such an awful thing."

"You really believe that?"

"It's better than being afraid," Sam told her, his voice quiet in the cold air. "Are you afraid?"

"Yes," Annie sighed, and then she seemed to hold her breath. The dark snow of the igloo held them like a grave. "No, it's…" her words broke off. Sam thought to ask a question but just waited. "My father died in the snow, frozen."

"On the tundra?"

"No, down south. He was drunk, coming home late from a bar. I was with my brothers and sisters, waiting, and he never came home."

"Is that why you came here?" Sam asked.

"After he died, I started arguing with my mother all the time. I guess I got into the wrong group at school. And then there was this guy." Her voice trailed off for a while. Then she gave a little laugh. "That guy even looked like Connor, and *he* was a jerk, too."

If there'd been more light, Sam could have seen Annie smile. As it was, the two of them sat silently in the semidarkness, both staring out the small entry hole to the igloo. Outside, the Northern Lights were putting on their show: the ancients playing soccer in the sky. Inside, the two teenagers sat beside each other, trying to share each other's warmth.

"I guess sending me up here was supposed to make things different, but I hate it," Annie said. "Everybody tells stories about me."

"That's because people don't really know you," Sam said. "If they did…"

"Then they'd know how messed up I am," she broke in.

Sam searched for words, some clumsy words to say what was in his mind. "Then they'd know who you really are. The way you always stand by your friends, and you don't give up hope, and you're so ..." Sam was going to say "pretty," but he stopped before the word came out. There were just too many words coming from his heart. When he'd spoken like this before to girls, they'd made fun of him.

"Do you like me, Sam?" Annie asked, her voice almost a whisper.

Sam nodded, and then realized she couldn't see him in the dark. "Yes," he said, his voice catching in his throat.

"I'm glad," Annie told him. "I've never met anyone like you before. You don't make a joke out of everything, like the kids I used to hang with. You're different."

Sam found that he couldn't talk at all, that his voice had gone silent. Did Annie mean she liked him and liked who he was? Or did it mean nothing at all? Words seemed as awkward as snow blocks hacked out in a blizzard.

Beside them, Connor stirred in his sleep. "No!" he shouted, his legs jerking suddenly. Then he, too, was awake.

"Did somebody come for us?" Connor asked.

"There's nobody yet," Annie told him, sounding groggy.

"Sam," Connor said.

"Yeah."

"I can't feel my arm anymore. Do you think that maybe it's frostbite? Are they going to have to cut it off?"

"I think it's broken and you're probably in shock, that's all," Sam told him. "We'll be rescued soon enough. The sun is starting to come up now."

"I'm freezing," Connor moaned.

Sam could see the steam from Connor's breath in the dim light of daybreak. It was a little above freezing in the igloo, but that meant it was forty degrees warmer than it was outside. "You're probably warmer than you were when we found you," Sam said.

"Face it, Connor, you're just scared, like some frightened little rabbit," Annie told him.

"Me?" Connor shot back. "No, not me. I'm just a little, you know."

"You're just full of yourself," Annie said bitterly. "You'd think you were God's gift to the north, racing around on your snowmobile, the big guy at school. But let things get tough, and then the real guy shows through. The real guy is scared stiff."

"Annie, come on," Connor pleaded.

"You know what I've figured out?" Annie went on. "I figured out that I'm better than you are. I don't have to cover up your bragging and your stupid smuggling. I can get through the night up here without whining and blubbering like a baby."

"Yeah, well listen, princess. Just keep your mouth shut or you'll be in as much trouble as me, whatever happens after this," Connor shot back.

Sam looked at the two of them, these two lost souls. They wanted so much they could never have and ignored what was already theirs: the land, the traditions, the people.

But that didn't mean they couldn't change.

Maybe if Sam could reach out and get over his shyness, he could do something for them. At least he could help Annie, who *wanted* to change, and maybe Connor, too. Connor had seen the face of death. Maybe he'd come close enough to want to change himself before he had to stare at death again.

"Annie, Connor," Sam said, "look at what the sun did."

He pointed to the wall of their makeshift igloo, at a spot of sunlight on the white wall. The sun, shining through the entrance hole, had given them a blaze of light.

"Look at that," Annie cried. "It's beautiful." In the morning light, Sam could see the smile on her face. And he felt his heart skip a beat.

"Yeah, I guess it is," Connor admitted. "So it means that somebody will come find us?"

"Maybe it means that things are going to be different," Sam said. "A new day, a new sun, a new life." His words trailed off into embarrassed silence. But this time no one laughed at him. Annie and Connor just listened and nodded their heads.

# CHAPTER 10

"It's a plane!" Annie shouted. "Somebody's looking for us!"

Sam crawled out of the igloo first, and then Annie came into the reddish light of dawn. Up over their heads, in the clear sky, was a small plane.

The two of them jumped up, waving and running so they could be seen against the snow. And then the plane tipped its wings.

"They saw us," Annie cried.

By this time, Connor, too, had climbed out of the shelter. He was shivering from the cold, and perhaps a fever, but the sight of the plane would keep him going.

The Search and Rescue team came in just twenty minutes. They arrived on three snowmobiles, with food and hot coffee. In another half-hour, the snowmobiles had brought them all back to town. They stopped first at Connor's house, where a police car was already parked. Then the Search and Rescue team took Annie and Sam to Sam's house. Both families—and one good friend—were waiting there.

Billy smiled as Sam came to the door. "You'll do anything to avoid that history project, won't you?" He slapped his friend on the back and laughed.

"So, did you finish the project while I was out there risking frostbite?" Sam asked.

"No way," Billy said. "I figured you'd be back soon enough. What happened to the three of you out there, anyway?"

Sam thought through it all: the storm, the search, finding Connor, losing the dogs, building a shelter, the long, cold night. But all he could say right then was, "I think I made a friend."

Billy looked at him for a moment, and then smiled when he figured out what Sam meant.

The older men looked hard at Sam and Annie. They wanted some answers.

"How did you fall off the *komatik*?" Grandfather Titus asked, shaking his head. "A hunter shouldn't fall off a sled, and *never* in a blizzard."

"There was a rock I didn't see," Sam explained.

"You go out to save this boy and almost get the three of you killed," said Annie's uncle, Josiah Amarook. He looked stern. "This is not good. And no one knew where you'd gone."

Sam looked at Annie—it was for her to speak up. "I didn't tell you," she said, looking down at the floor. "I didn't want anyone to know about Connor and his secret camp."

"Search and Rescue found the camp before they found you," Grandfather Titus explained. "The police are talking to Connor's father now. I think they've suspected something for a long time."

"How much did you know, Annie?" her uncle asked, his face tired and drawn.

"I knew enough," she said. "But I couldn't tell. I was so stupid."

For the first time in the whole ordeal, Sam saw

Annie cry. The tears that ran down her cheeks were not tears of pain, or relief, or gratitude. They were tears of shame.

"Annie," said her uncle, "you might be happier back down in the south."

But Annie cut him off. "No!" she cried. "No, not after all this. I was wrong. I admit it. But don't send me back now. I'll take whatever punishment you want to give, but I don't want to go back."

Her uncle spoke slowly. "You said you don't trust us. You said you couldn't tell us the truth. You've said again and again that you have no friends here. So, why do you want to stay?"

"Because things are different now," Annie replied, glancing at Sam. "Now I've got a *reason* to stay." ■

Published in the United States of America by:

**ꝓ Dominie Press, Inc.**

1949 Kellogg Avenue
Carlsbad, California 92008 USA

www.dominie.com

ISBN 0-7685-2353-2
Printed in Singapore by PH Productions Pte Ltd
1 2 3 4 5 PH 08 07 06 05 04